Reflections of Messiah

Reflections
of Messiah

Contemporary Advent Meditations
Inspired by Handel

Jim Melchiorre

UPPER
ROOM BOOKS®
NASHVILLE

REFLECTIONS OF MESSIAH
Contemporary Advent Meditations Inspired by Handel
© Copyright 2003 by Jim Melchiorre
All rights reserved.

The Upper Room® Web site: www.upperroom.org

Cover Design: Ed Maksimowicz
Cover Illustration: Natalie Cox
Interior Design and Layout: Nancy J. Cole-Hatcher
Interior Illustrations: Jim Osborn
First Printing: 2003
Printed in the United States of America

Library of Congress Cataloging-in-Publication Data
Melchiorre, Jim, 1952–
Reflections of Messiah : contemporary Advent meditations inspired by
    Handel / Jim Melchiorre.
    p. cm.
ISBN 0-8358-9856-3
1. Advent—Meditations. 2. Handel, George Frideric, 1685–1759. Messiah. I. Title.
    BV40.M45 2003
    242'.332—dc21   2003004630

To
Alice Marie Doosey Melchiorre
1922–2000

CONTENTS

FOURTH WEEK OF ADVENT

PREFACE
～

In the Cathedral of Saints Peter and Paul in Llandaff,
Wales, there is a marker bearing these words:

> Be attentive to the times of the day. We live in the
> fullness of time. Every moment is God's own good
> time.

I believe that many of life's events occur exactly
when they are supposed to—in the fullness of time. This
book required an extremely lengthy gestation period. It
began as an almost daily journal in 1997 after I resolved
to observe Advent more intentionally. The journal
entries and other notes then sat in limbo for at least two
years until my wife, Cheryl, and I finally acquiesced to
modern technology and bought a compact disc player,
as well as a CD of Handel's *Messiah*.

Listening to the oratorio, reading the scriptures on
which *Messiah* is based, and some inexplicable inspira-
tion led me to the idea of exploring the message of
Messiah for contemporary American society.

Stories of people I have met throughout my journalism career comprise a large part of what you're about

to read. This book is also a journal. I wrote some entries as early as December 1997 and others as late as the summer of 2002. Those entries reflect the time in which they were written and attempt to honor that moment while still offering the reader a transcendent relevance.

The events of September 11, 2001, occurred as I was writing this book. Especially because I live in New York City, the emotions and insights sparked by that day provide a basis for several meditations.

The book's central theme is the radical mission of the Messiah. Understanding this mission can transform us personally and recruit us for the work of transforming the world.

I hope that use of this book as a devotional guide during Advent will inspire readers to maintain the integrity of this wonderful four-week period of reflection and repentance—rather than to view this time as a monthlong shopping spree for Christmas.

Not long ago I learned of a custom at Saint Bede Abbey in Peru, Illinois: The monks there cannot put up any decorations until Christmas Eve. I'd like to see that tradition, an old one that has fallen out of favor, spread more widely in our consumeristic culture.

HOW TO USE THIS BOOK

Advent can run as short as twenty-two days or as long as twenty-nine. This book provides enough daily chapters to cover the longest Advent season. Feel free to adjust your own devotional schedule as you see fit.

Most scripture verses used in this book come from Handel's oratorio; they were chosen by Handel's collaborator, Charles Jennens. I added several verses that do not appear in *Messiah* because they seemed relevant to the reflection for a particular date. Whenever I made such additions, I noted that in the daily meditation.

Most scripture quotations are from the New Revised Standard Version, considered by the publisher and many Bible scholars, seminaries, and divinity schools to be the most accurate translation from the ancient Hebrew and Greek. However, I must mention that Handel used the King James Version in writing *Messiah*. So, if you are a fan of the oratorio and can hum the music and sing some of the words from memory, don't be alarmed to see "Every valley shall be exalted" (Isa. 40:4) become "Every valley shall be lifted up."

Each daily meditation includes a brief prayer and questions that can be used with a discussion group or as a starting point for keeping a personal journal.

Finally, always remember that the reflections, thoughts, insights, and opinions presented in this book represent one person—the author. Feel free to agree, debate, or outright reject. That's the only proper relationship between a writer and reader.

Shalom!

First Week
OF
Advent

SUNDAY

~

Comfort Zones

Comfort, O comfort my people, says your God.
Speak tenderly to Jerusalem.

ISAIAH 40:1-2

Emerging from our apartment building one Sunday morning, I glimpsed an elderly man walking with a cane, crossing the street at 79th Street and York Avenue. The weather was cold and breezy, and he was bent and frail. It occurred to me that simply crossing the street with his cane was an ambitious task. Yet I noticed he was trying to pick up a coin from the street, his right hand on the cane and his left hand stretched out, dangling, reaching toward the pavement. He looked awfully precarious to me.

About eighty years old and reasonably well-dressed, the man wore a tie and a fedora. I wondered how badly he needed that coin. Was he broke or just practicing a lifelong habit of thrift?

Later that morning, I watched as an elderly woman, buffeted by a cold wind, tried to hail a cab. Then, even later, walking up from the subway on the Upper West Side of Manhattan, hit with the familiar smells of the city, I thought of the thousands of people who move through our lives and our society lonely, unnoticed, anonymous. And how most of us try so hard to avoid contact with those who are old or idiosyncratic or who smell different or whose skin is darker or lighter.

We treasure our comfort zones. Not only creature comforts but also, especially, the psychic comforts we associate with the familiar.

So what should we make of this word *comfort* during a season in which we anticipate the arrival of the Messiah? Perhaps we should embrace the word *comfort* when used as a verb—and remain cautious when it's used as a noun.

Certainly the work of the Messiah calls us to comfort the old, the weak, the marginalized, the oppressed, and the homeless, who may smell bad because they're sleeping on the streets, under bridges, and on subway platforms. If we heed the call, we're almost certain to surrender some of our own comfort.

It's been said before, but it's terribly relevant at this season of the year: The work of the Messiah always has involved comforting the afflicted—and afflicting the comfortable. If we truly want to follow that Messiah, as we say we do, then our work is clearly the same.

PRAYER

All-knowing and all-seeing God, open our eyes to all that goes on around us. Heighten our sensitivity to persons living on the margins—those children of yours who are so visible yet whom we often fail to see.

REFLECTION

1. It's a fairly normal human instinct to feel most comfortable in familiar surroundings with familiar people. How do we overcome that tendency in order to minister to persons on the margins?

2. What do you think about the statement that the Messiah's work always has involved afflicting the comfortable? What comforts might you need to sacrifice to participate in the Messiah's work?

MONDAY

A Lot on Our Plates

Every valley shall be lifted up,
*   and every mountain and hill be made low;*
the uneven ground shall become level,
*   and the rough places a plain.*

ISAIAH 40:4

Uh-oh. Hearing this verse won't encourage people to feel happy or tranquil at Christmastime. Instead, this scripture sounds like a way to turn the world upside down. And a lot of believers think that's the exact intent.

The Reverend Jim Lewis, an Episcopal priest, believes that more prayers, blessings, and graces are said over chicken than any other food. Considering the popularity of chicken, not only at church suppers and picnics but also in the diet of many Americans, Lewis may be correct. When we give thanks for that poultry, Lewis wants us to think hard about what we're doing.

"To thank God for this wonderful gift and the fact that it's feeding us, without looking beneath the surface of that grace to see the curse out there for so many people bringing that food to us, is blasphemous," he says.

Lewis now lives in West Virginia. I first met him in Delaware, where he led the Delmarva Poultry Justice Alliance, a movement aimed at improving the lives of slaughterhouse employees. Latinos who are recent immigrants to the United States comprise a majority of that work force.

Lewis not only tried to improve the living conditions of poultry workers but also worked to organize them into labor unions, believing that only in unity can there be strength. And, by the way, he doesn't believe in objectivity. Lewis takes sides.

"The power [of the poultry industry] is so great, and the impotence of those who work in the industry so meager, that the church and the religious community must take a side in order for there to be some balance," he claims.

People often say that religion and politics don't mix. Perhaps what they're really saying is that such a mix makes all of us uncomfortable, despite where we stand on religion and politics.

"I was raised to stay out of trouble, to not offend anybody, and to make sure everybody's happy," Lewis says. "That was a lie, in terms of the gospel."

Lewis attributes his involvement in labor activism to his reading of scripture:

- in Isaiah;
- in the four Gospels, which record the life, work, and teachings of Jesus; and
- in the Hebrew Scriptures in the books named after prophets, such as Amos and Hosea. (We sometimes call them the Minor Prophets, but from my perspective their message is of major importance.)

The Bible contains revolutionary truths—if we'd truly practice its teachings. We don't often associate upheaval and social change with the quiet, reflective season of Advent, but maybe we should.

PRAYER

Creator God, slow us down as we eat our meals. Challenge us to think of those who labor so that we might eat. Remind us that our blessings should not come at the expense of any of your children.

REFLECTION

1. When was the last time you paused before eating to consider the food on your plate and how it got there? How can we better appreciate that all we take for granted is truly a gift, brought to us through the goodness of God, God's creation, and the hard work of people we rarely see?

2. What moral responsibility, if any, do you think Americans bear for immigrants who work in low-paying, often dangerous jobs that make it possible for us to enjoy an enviable standard of living?

3. In your opinion, do labor unions serve as a positive or negative influence in making our society more moral and ethical? Explain.

TUESDAY

∼

Acting Like We Own the Place

For thus says the LORD of hosts: Once again, in a little while, I will shake the heavens and the earth and the sea and the dry land; and I will shake all the nations, so that the treasure of all nations shall come, and I will fill this house with splendor, says the LORD of hosts.

HAGGAI 2:6-7

These verses from Haggai suggest dramatic action initiated by God—shaking the heavens and earth and all nations. In reality, this scripture deals not with destruction but with construction of the second temple after the exile of the Israelites in Babylon. I found verse 8 of this passage most thought-provoking: "The silver is mine, and the gold is mine, says the LORD of hosts."

Those words made me think of the way many Americans view property and possessions, ownership and stewardship. Then I remembered the words of Melvin Grey Owl.

I met Grey Owl, an elder of the Crow Creek Dakota tribe in South Dakota, during a Volunteers in Mission trip in June 1998. One evening as his grandchildren performed a circle dance for us, Grey Owl spoke of many issues, including the philosophical differences between his nineteenth-century ancestors and the westward-bound settlers who took over their land and put the native people on reservations. The settlers saw land as a prize to be won, owned, and possessed. But in Crow Creek Dakota theology, that view makes no sense.

The Crow Creek Dakota asks: "How can you own land? Can you own the sky?" I see a connection between the words of Haggai and the philosophy of the Crow Creek Dakota as explained by Melvin Grey Owl.

Our time on this earth is frightfully short. We follow forebears from tens of thousands of years ago, and most likely generations of descendants will follow us. We get a brief chance to coexist thoughtfully with the creation—or to abuse it.

Families may remain on the same land for decades, even centuries. They pass it on to their children and grandchildren. They may hold a piece of paper that says it's their "property." But do they really own it?

If we stop to consider the Crow Creek Dakota perspective, the phrase "owning land" seems almost ludicrous. Yet this concept is a cultural construction in which many people have great emotional investment.

In writing this, I realize I'm walking on thin ice because I appear to be questioning private ownership of land. What I am suggesting is that we philosophically consider the bigger picture—the millennia that came before our lifetimes and the many years that likely will follow our time on earth. We are stewards with a short-term lease.

Many Native Americans—and more than a few white pioneers—shed their blood and lost their lives in a fight for land. Today the same battle rages between Arabs and Israelis on land they have alternately shared, disputed, and bled over for forty centuries.

Land has often stood in the way of peace, justice, equality, and community—in short, it has stood in the way of the work of the Messiah. It will continue to do so—until we redefine the word *ours*.

PRAYER

God of eternity, how you must shake your head at our arrogance toward your creation, which predates us and will endure long after we're gone. Grant us the perspective to remember that we're only short-term renters, and help us to stop acting like we own the place.

REFLECTION

1. If your family has owned land for a long time and passed it down from generation to generation, explain what that land means to you.

2. What do you think about Mount Rushmore, a mountain containing the carved faces of dead white presidents and situated in the heart of land sacred to Native Americans?

3. The Israelis claim the Holy Land as their birthright from God. The Arabs say they've lived there continuously for four thousand years and want to remain. How do you regard this bloody, seemingly endless fight over land?

WEDNESDAY

~

Troublemakers

Then the glory of the LORD shall be revealed,
and all people shall see it together,
for the mouth of the LORD has spoken.

ISAIAH 40:5

My wife, Cheryl, our youngest son, Mark, and I received a great surprise late one winter day in New York City. Our friends Elizabeth and Peter Storey had come to New York for a bishops' conference. A former bishop of the Methodist Church in South Africa, Peter spent a year as interim pastor of Calvary United Methodist Church in Nashville. Our family held membership in this congregation a few years ago.

When I learned that Peter and Elizabeth could visit with us for a couple of hours, I invited our current pastor, the Reverend James Karpen (better known as "K") from Saint Paul and Saint Andrew United Methodist Church in Manhattan, to join us.

These two pastors know each other and share the experience of living in South Africa during apartheid. Peter spent most of his life in ministry fighting for equality and justice against that oppressive system in which a white minority held all power over the majority population of blacks. K had visited South Africa as a young man, before he went to seminary, as an employee of a not-for-profit organization attempting to end the apartheid system by exposing American companies that cooperated with it.

One brief exchange in the conversation between Peter and K caught my attention and seared itself into my memory. K mentioned that when he visited South Africa in 1982, he was ordered to swear that he was not working for the Methodist Church. (K has been an active Methodist for most of his life.) Peter laughed and said he was surprised that anyone with any Methodist connection would even be allowed into South Africa at that time.

To the powerful in South Africa, being a Methodist meant you were a troublemaker; your presence potentially threatened the unjust system. Being a Methodist meant that your loyalty to preserving the status quo could not be trusted. Being a Methodist meant that you would most likely align yourself with the poor, the powerless, the marginalized.

All that made me think about what message others

receive when we say we're Methodist or Catholic or Lutheran or Christian. Do those names label us as troublemakers, threats to entrenched powers, unmistakable allies of the poor and the weak? Or do we fit right into our culture and try to keep everybody comfortable?

If the work of the Messiah really is to transform the world—to turn society upside down, to raise the valleys, lower the hills, straighten the crooked paths, and smooth over the rough roads—can anyone identify us as the Messiah's coworkers?

If not, why not?

PRAYER

God in heaven, we know that we should spend our time on earth living as responsible citizens. Help us to remain mindful of that but also to remember that our ultimate loyalty must be to you and your gospel.

REFLECTION

1. Some people say religion and politics should not mix. In what ways do you agree with this assertion? In what ways do you disagree?

2. Cite an example in your life when your nation's government pursued a policy that violated the deepest tenets of your faith. How did you feel and react?

3. Someone has said that faith is always a personal matter, but that does not mean faith must be a *private* matter. What does that statement mean to you in terms of living out the gospel message?

THURSDAY

A Gentle Threat

> *But who can endure the day of his coming, and*
> *who can stand when he appears?*
>   *For he is like a refiner's fire and like fullers'*
> *[launderers'] soap.*

MALACHI 3:2

Who will be standing as God enters the room? Not I. I'll be on my knees. If we believe in God and think that we'll eventually have to face that God and account for the life we have lived—well, that's a sobering thought. Enough to make almost any of us a little reflective and humble.

Indeed, what account can we give of our lives? During my journalism career, I have met many people who, from all appearances, probably could make a pretty good report on Judgment Day—they have devoted their lives to causes in which they believe.

Sister Marge Eilerman of the Order of Saint Francis stood outside a bus on the grounds of the U.S. Army post at Fort Benning, near Columbus, Georgia, while I covered a protest demonstration as a reporter for the Odyssey Cable Channel. Authorities had just arrested Eilerman and several hundred other people for trespassing on government property as they staged their annual vigil of opposition to the School of the Americas. Protesters blame the school for educating Latin American military officers who have often gone back home and committed atrocities against civilians.

Okay, so now we've typecast Marge as a peace activist. That's a valid label, but it hardly explains the full story. I later learned that Marge's strong opposition to the school stems at least in part from her own experiences as a missionary in Mexico and Central America.

Fine. Now we've got her figured out. *Liberal-leaning Catholic sister doing mission work among Spanish-speaking peasants far from the borders of the United States.*

Wrong again.

The next time I saw Marge, we were in Booneville, Kentucky. Eilerman lived and worked in Appalachia for twenty-one years. In Booneville, she taught evangelism classes, ran a weekly clothing sale, started the community's first Catholic parish, and even opened a factory that makes furniture from old plastic milk jugs.

The people in Booneville look quite different from the campesinos of Latin America. Everybody in Booneville is white; most are Protestant; and they can't make a living growing crops, so many work in mines.

In reality, however, the miners of Appalachia and the campesinos of Latin America are not that different. Both groups are poor, marginalized, and exploited.

Six months later, in August 1998, I watch Sister Marge again, this time at a cathedral in Lexington, Kentucky. The guest of honor tonight, she is making her last public appearance before heading off to federal prison for her part in the ongoing Fort Benning protest.

A woman in her sixties, a Catholic sister, tossed behind bars in a federal prison for vandalizing U.S. property. What's going on here? She hardly represents a danger to society.

But wait a minute. Eilerman publicly stands up and attacks a U.S. military policy. She works among the poor, first in Mexico and Central America and then in the mountains of central Kentucky. More than that, she lives among the poor, becomes their voice.

Now she's willing to go to prison for her beliefs. This particular evening, Sister Marge tells those gathered in the church, "If civil disobedience is practiced in a prayerful spirit of nonviolent love, it takes on the nature of a sacrament."

Sister Marge represents no physical threat, but upon further reflection, I guess she really is dangerous, just as Amos, Hosea, and John the Baptist were dangerous. Just as that baby born in Bethlehem was dangerous.

Come to think of it, the Messiah's message and work remain dangerous to this day. Dangerous—and necessary.

PRAYER

Good and gracious God, the poor, the forgotten, the marginalized are all colors, speak all languages, and live everywhere. They're living close to us right now. Open our eyes to see them—and open our hearts to act as advocates for justice.

REFLECTION

1. How are the peasants of Latin America and the coal miners of Appalachia, so different at first glance, really kindred spirits?

2. Sister Marge speaks of civil disobedience as a sacrament. Does that statement strike you as true—or blasphemous? Why?

3. Some would say that nuns, priests, ministers, and missionaries should work to save souls, not protest against the government. How do you see the role of these disciples of Christ? What do you see as the role of laypeople?

FRIDAY

∾

The Jesus Train

*Therefore the Lord himself will give you a sign.
Look, the young woman is with child and shall bear
a son, and shall name him Immanuel.*

ISAIAH 7:14

I saw a poster today for a play called *Jesus Jumped the A
Train*. Perhaps that image is powerful only to a New
Yorker. The A train travels about as far as any subway
line in the city. It begins in Inwood, at the northwest tip
of Manhattan, then moves south through Washington
Heights and Harlem. A song called "Take the A Train"
became the signature tune of Duke Ellington's band, and
its title made a lot of sense because Ellington lived in the
Sugar Hill section of Harlem and played his unforget-
table music along 125th Street. The A train would have
been his subway route of choice.

After leaving Harlem, the A train continues down
the west side of Manhattan, then into Brooklyn and

eventually Queens, ending at Far Rockaway, practically on the shore of the Atlantic Ocean.

If Jesus were ministering in New York City as the itinerant preacher he was, he would undoubtedly hop the A train and stand or sit among the great diversity of people who live in this city.

Black people, white people, people wearing suits, homeless folks sleeping on subway platforms in the winter.

Hispanics, Albanians, Koreans, Chinese.

Muslims fasting for Ramadan, Jews keeping kosher. Unwed mothers, HIV-positive people, AIDS patients.

Older teens just out of school, younger teens skipping class. Senior citizens scrunched up in the train seat, their threadbare clothing scarcely keeping them warm.

The work of the Messiah includes them all.

Retired Bishop Peter Storey of South Africa believes that God offers us a personal relationship but not a private salvation deal. Storey says we can't domesticate Jesus—take him home and claim him for our family, neighborhood, denomination, or country.

In New York City, Jesus jumped the A train. In Georgia, look for him in a pickup truck. In Havana, I'll bet you'll find him in front of the government ration store with the old man who shows up to get bread and sees the loaf cut into thirds before he gets his allotment.

Perhaps we should rethink our ideas about the next coming of Christ. Maybe he's already here.

PRAYER

Almighty God, remind us never to claim you exclusively for our culture, our tradition, or our nationality. Help us recognize your transcendence that unites people from all nations and backgrounds in your family.

REFLECTION

1. If you belong to a faith community, consider candidly how open your congregation would be to an influx of diverse people as described in this meditation.

2. How comfortable would you feel about attending a religious service in a synagogue if you're Christian or Muslim? in a mosque if you're Jewish or Christian? in a church if you're Muslim or Jewish?

SATURDAY

~

Charity and Justice

He will sit as a refiner and purifier of silver, and he will purify the descendants of Levi and refine them like gold and silver, until they present offerings to the LORD in righteousness.

MALACHI 3:3

Today I read a column by our former pastor, Reverend Peter van Eys, of Calvary United Methodist Church in Nashville. As I try to focus my mind this Advent on the theme of the Messiah's work of radical change, Peter's words make me quite uncomfortable.

The column includes this trenchant sentence: "Churches need poor people around in order to be involved in charity rather than justice."

Wow. Just when we started feeling good about ourselves, about those Christmas food drives we've organized, those Salvation Army Angel Tree gifts we've bought for needy children, that check we just mailed out to the umpteenth charity requesting our help.

Surely working for charity is important, isn't it? All that time, money, and energy expended. What kind of thanks is Peter's statement for all our efforts?

Maybe we react so passionately because Peter's words are true. Working for justice is infinitely tougher than working for charity, as necessary as both are. Working for justice is also much more dangerous because it makes us far more vulnerable.

Providing food and shelter for the homeless makes nobody really uncomfortable. Publicly challenging the system that leaves those people on the street—well, that's going to step on some toes.

Charity work must never go away. Like a triage unit in a hospital, charity addresses the immediate crisis. Charity is part of the Messiah's work. So is justice. Working for justice means working for changes. Glacial and rapid changes.

I doubt that God will judge us harshly for not immediately achieving dramatic results in our work for justice. I think God may show more concern over those times we haven't even tried.

PRAYER

Creator of all, this business of justice and charity is tricky and difficult for us. You know the proper balance; help us discern it.

Reflection

1. What do you think of the statement "Charity is a gift; justice is a right"?

2. How do you think faith communities should respond to government invitations to become involved in social work? At what point can the church's efforts for justice be compromised?

Second Week
OF
Advent

SUNDAY

∽

An Uncommon Community of Faith

Get you up to a high mountain,
  O Zion, herald of good tidings;
lift up your voice with strength,
  O Jerusalem, herald of good tidings,
  lift it up, do not fear;
say to the cities of Judah,
  "Here is your God!"

ISAIAH 40:9

Gary Huber recalls his first encounter with the Reverend Deborah Little: "I heard her say, 'Come, I've got good news. Sit down.'" Huber, a homeless, part-time carpenter, often lives in a pickup truck, a condemned building, or, his personal favorite, the woods of southern New Hampshire.

Reverend Little, an Episcopal priest, leads a "congregation without walls" that has met on the Boston

43

Common since 1996. She left her job as director of communications for Harvard Law School to go to seminary, then hit the streets as a priest to the homeless.

The members of Debbie Little's congregation keep on coming to the outdoor service through the heat and humidity of summer and the snow, wind, and ice of a Boston winter, because as street people they rarely enter a building for any reason.

"Buildings have assumptions," Little says, half smiling, adding that her parishioners "are very conscious of how they smell, how they dress, and how they look." Little knows perfectly well that buildings are inanimate objects that cannot make assumptions, smell odor, or see the clothes of the human beings who inhabit them. Instead Little is speaking of the usual reaction of many church people to the homeless.

"Privileged people's worship is simply not what I understand to be the gospel of Jesus Christ," Little says. "I don't think Jesus is being sentimental or casual when he sends us to the poor to learn of God. I think he means it literally that the table is just not his if it doesn't include the poor."

The story of Debbie Little and her ministry at Common Cathedral offers us material for reflection during the Advent season when we wait for a Messiah who is aligned with the poor and committed to justice.

Little remembers the day she felt inexorably drawn to begin her street ministry. "I was just thinking about

Jesus, and my next thought was, 'Wham! The church is out here!' Jesus went where the *people* were, not where the buildings were. It just felt so simple and so clear."

Scripture demonstrates that Jesus spent a lot of time with the poor. He also ate more than a couple of meals with people of privilege in society. In both settings his message stayed consistent.

Debbie Little follows Christ's example. Many Sunday mornings she preaches in wealthy suburban churches, talking about the ministry she will renew later that day on the Boston Common. Little says she's happy to serve as a link between two worlds.

With Jesus as her example, Little keeps her message consistent, whether she's talking with the wealthy or the poor. How else could she be a force for reconciliation, a laborer doing the work of the Messiah?

PRAYER

God of all people, keep us from making our church buildings the subject of idolatry when they should be open doors to your reconciliation and love.

REFLECTION

1. What assumptions might your church make if half a dozen homeless people walked in the doors at 10:45 A.M. next Sunday?

2. Little has written that "the middle- and upper-class order of things must be broken open." How do you feel about this statement?

3. What parallels do you see between Reverend Little and another priest of the same tradition, John Wesley, who took the gospel to the countryside during the eighteenth century?

Monday

∿

Behind Bars

For a child has been born for us,
  a son given to us;
authority rests upon his shoulders;
and he is named Wonderful Counselor,
  Mighty God,
  Everlasting Father, Prince of Peace.
        Isaiah 9:6

Christmas is fast approaching, and I'm traveling pretty quickly myself, driving a rental car north on the New Jersey Turnpike between Philadelphia and New York. I'm listening to the radio as Scott Simon of NPR's *Weekend Edition Saturday* interviews Colonel Margaret Hay of the Salvation Army, the chaplain at Rochester Prison in Kent, England. In December 2000, Hay won the Preacher of the Year Award from the *Times* of London.

At Simon's request, Hay reads from her award-winning sermon, which describes a visit to a prisoner, "another young man hibernating in hell, sleeping away his sorrow."

The image of a prisoner sitting behind bars is not the most popular image at Christmastime. We'd rather see little children surrounding Santa Claus. Or a rosy-cheeked baby lying in a manger with well-washed, clean-shaven shepherds joining Mary and Joseph in a kneeling, contemplative pose.

Hay reminds us in her sermon that "The Christ child, 'pink and white with cheeks so rosy' as we used to sing at school, is also the wild warrior battling for his beloved world." The Messiah, fighting for those "people who walked in darkness [who] have seen a great light" (Isa. 9:2). Those people represent all of us, those of us behind bars and those who are not.

Hay's sermon continues, "The Word was a kindled flame, a sign of God's hope for that weeping man [in prison] and for the entire human community." Most of us don't like to think of *our* Messiah as being the same as a *prisoner's* Messiah. We don't like to think that the prisoner's need for that Messiah is identical to ours.

But Advent is an excellent time to remind ourselves that fundamentally we're all in the same boat.

As I speed northward, Scott Simon is back on the radio, speaking admiringly of Margaret Hay's sermon. Simon notes that Hay's prison ministry "makes the Word flesh." Which is, of course, the very definition of Incarnation.

PRAYER

God of the forgotten, the marginalized, and the trapped, may we be instruments of your love and reconciliation wherever and whenever they are needed.

REFLECTION

1. People in prison have been convicted; some of them may actually be guilty of a crime. How should Christians treat prisoners? What guidance does scripture provide for treatment of prisoners?

2. How do you feel about seeing yourself and a convicted prisoner as equals before God?

3. As we approach Christmas and see the proliferation of nativity scenes with a baby in a manger surrounded by simple, loving parents, how does Colonel Hay's description of the Christ child as a "wild warrior" make you feel?

TUESDAY

✎

A Traveler, Not a Tourist

Then the eyes of the blind shall be opened,
and the ears of the deaf unstopped;
then the lame shall leap like a deer,
and the tongue of the speechless sing for joy.
For waters shall break forth in the wilderness,
and streams in the desert.

ISAIAH 35:5-6

If I made a list of the ten people I most admire, Norris Allen of Dickson, Tennessee, would be on it. A building contractor and a former chemistry teacher, Norris never had a passport or figured he needed one until he was past forty. That's when his eyes were opened to the plight of others around the world.

In 1978 Norris joined a ministry called Volunteers in Mission that has since taken him on nearly fifty overseas trips to build schools, churches, homes, and community facilities for free. His first trip brought Norris to Belize, a country he'd never heard of. "I had a spiritual conviction there on that first trip when I saw how people had to live," Norris told me. "I had been struggling to find something meaningful in my life. Then I realized I had construction skills."

The Volunteers in Mission (VIM) movement swept me up when I made my first trip in 1986. Over the past decade and a half, I have traveled twice with Norris and seven times with other teams.

Many themes of *Messiah* resonate with veterans of VIM. Much of their work takes place in Central America and the Caribbean, areas where poverty has long existed, at least in part, because of exploitation by more powerful nations. Visiting such countries makes it much easier to understand why Christians in those nations see Jesus not only as Comforter but also as Liberator, the one who shakes the status quo of society to its roots, who truly does exalt the valleys, lower the mountains, straighten the crooked paths, and smooth the rough roads.

With the notable exception of African Americans, most of us in the United States do not embrace the image of Jesus as Liberator. We usually don't see the need for such radical change. After all, from where we sit, the world seems to be a pretty comfortable place. But not everybody sits in that same place. Statistically speaking, *most* of the world does not.

Along with the lesson of service to others, Norris Allen—and the rest of us in VIM—learned something else: Many people don't view the world from our privileged perspective. To them, the work of the Messiah remains incomplete. That Messiah beckons them to roll up their sleeves and get to work. The Messiah invites us to do the same.

PRAYER

Loving God, it is said that travel broadens our perspectives. Travel can also jar us into recognizing the reality of poverty and injustice. Use our travels to nudge us to join in the work of the Messiah.

REFLECTION

1. If you have traveled overseas, explore the feelings you experienced, especially in less developed countries, feelings such as sympathy, superiority, and gratitude.

2. Citizens of other nations sometimes use the phrase "ugly Americans" to describe U.S. tourists who want to stay only in chain hotels, eat bacon and eggs or other American foods for breakfast, and communicate only in English. Discuss this phenomenon.

WEDNESDAY

~

Room in the Inn

He will feed his flock like a shepherd;
*   he will gather the lambs in his arms,*
and carry them in his bosom,
*   and gently lead the mother sheep.*
                                    ISAIAH 40:11

A Messiah who gathers a flock and nourishes its lambs is a wonderful image of inclusion in a world where even people of goodwill often erect fences and barriers to exclude anyone different in language, skin color, income, or faith.

One of the great honors of my life was meeting and getting to know Reverend Charles Strobel, a Roman Catholic priest in Nashville, Tennessee. One winter back in the 1980s, Strobel noticed street people congregating in the parking lot of the church he pastored in a blue-collar neighborhood in East Nashville. The awful cold of that night worried Strobel. Quite on impulse, he opened the cafeteria of his church and let the homeless spend the night inside.

That experience led Strobel to brainstorm and organize what became known as Room in the Inn. For seventeen years, more than a hundred congregations have opened their doors one night a week to provide a hot meal, warm overnight shelter, breakfast, showers, sack lunches, and, most important, *hospitality* to guests who live in a different world within their own city.

At first Strobel had a difficult time convincing congregations to use their places of worship as homeless shelters. People felt great affection for their church buildings, and those emotional attachments made them want, at least subliminally, to protect their churches from exposure to an unknown population, a group of people who look, dress, and smell different.

Strobel asks: "Could the protection and beautification of our place of worship be a symbol of an unwillingness to risk, not as individual believers, but as communities of faith? By limiting our activities there to programs that are safe, do we as a congregation believe that we will be secure in our faith?"

Even those committed to the work of the Messiah—who believe that serving the poor, the marginalized, and the despised is the heart of the gospel message—might at first be more comfortable serving homeless people in a municipal shelter than in their home church or synagogue.

We love our places of worship just as we love our other "stuff." And we keep trying to soften the message of the Messiah so that we don't have to change our church buildings—or ourselves.

It doesn't work. Charlie Strobel points out that until after 300 C.E. there is no record of any building associated with Christianity. The biggest growth in the faith occurred when believers had no roof over their heads other than homes, isolated caves, or the occasional borrowed room. Strobel observes, "The willingness of believers to risk everything—property and possessions, status and rank, even their own lives—for the sake of the gospel was the spring that watered the seeds of faith."

Room in the Inn has provided the benefits of hospitality—shelter, food, clothing, rest—to thousands of street people over the past seventeen years. Those who serve the nightly guests have learned a lot. Perhaps the greatest lesson is realizing the need to loose themselves from emotional attachment to buildings so that they can be consumed with the liberating passion of doing the Messiah's work.

PRAYER

Eternal God, scripture teaches us the lesson of hospitality early on, at least as early as the visit of the three strangers to the tent of Sarah and Abraham. Help us remember that the lesson still stands.

REFLECTION

1. Churches face the danger of resembling country clubs, admitting only members who look, think, and live alike. How can we recognize that danger and prevent it from happening?

2. On the other hand, what is our responsibility as good stewards of a building and facilities for which the congregation has made sacrifices to build?

THURSDAY

❦

Jesus in the Mirror?

*The next day he [John the Baptist] saw Jesus com-
ing toward him and declared, "Here is the Lamb of
God who takes away the sin of the world!"*

JOHN 1:29

A friend of mine, photojournalist Lyle Jackson, pro-
duced a television documentary called *Picture-
Perfect Jesus*. Its subject was a 1940 painting by Warner
Sallman called *Head of Christ*, which became America's
most popular image of Jesus Christ during the twentieth
century. The oil portrait shows Jesus in profile and portrays him with light brown hair, blue eyes, and an angu-
lar face.

The painting reassured people of many generations.
Reproductions appeared everywhere, from funeral fans
to clocks and calendars. GIs even received wallet-sized
copies of the painting at their induction, along with
their vaccinations and dog tags.

The image particularly comforted people of European descent. No wonder. This Jesus looks like them.

Of course, it's ludicrous to imagine that a Jewish man living in first-century Palestine would look like that. A former colleague of mine, columnist Tony Norman of the *Pittsburgh Post-Gazette*, jokingly calls the image *Jesus of Norway*.

Fundamentally, there's probably nothing wrong with ethnocentric views of Jesus because if there is one lesson we should learn from the Incarnation, it's that God wants to be among us. African-American believers often display pictures of a black Jesus, an image that sometimes sparks a double take from whites—and protests from the more bigoted.

Oh, how we long for Jesus to make us feel comfortable. How deeply we desire for Jesus to be like us.

But Jesus does look like us—all of us. What we must do is expand our perception of "us." And, while we're at it, we need to do one more thing. Instead of wishing so sincerely for Jesus to be like us, we can work harder at being like him.

PRAYER

God in heaven, you clearly want to be among us—Jesus proves that. May we feel kinship with all your children, who are surely our sisters and brothers.

REFLECTION

1. Why do you think we see so many pictures portraying Jesus with fair hair and blue eyes?

2. In what ways has the dominant culture of various nations, often exported through colonialism and imperialism, forced an image of Jesus on people?

FRIDAY

❧

Banned from the Christmas Pageant

John said to the crowds that came out to be baptized by him, "You brood of vipers! Who warned you to flee from the wrath to come? Bear fruits worthy of repentance. Do not begin to say to yourselves, 'We have Abraham as our ancestor'; for I tell you, God is able from these stones to raise up children to Abraham. Even now the ax is lying at the root of the trees; every tree therefore that does not bear good fruit is cut down and thrown into the fire."

LUKE 3:7-9

The Reverend James Karpen, better known as "K," serves as pastor of Saint Paul and Saint Andrew United Methodist Church on Manhattan's Upper West Side in New York City. In the interest of full disclosure, Karpen is my pastor, and Cheryl, Mark, and I are members of that congregation.

A sermon Karpen preached in December 2000 touched on several important themes of Advent and the mission of the Messiah. For that reason, I included the scripture from Luke with this meditation even though it is not found in Handel's oratorio.

Karpen points out that John the Baptist never shows up in any of the traditional Christmas pageants and plays presented during Advent by churches and schools around the world. Karpen wonders why. Is it because "Advent is a peaceful, contemplative time of year, [and] John the Baptist has a way of causing trouble—a way of disturbing the peace? John comes on the scene demanding repentance, warning us to turn our lives around, to turn our lives upside down!"

I think one reason we like Advent is because, along with a sanitized view of the coming of the Christ child, it makes us quick to believe the lyrics of the beloved Christmas carol: "All is calm, all is bright." Karpen's sermon challenges us to see that John the Baptist also plays a role in the Messiah story.

We say that we love peace. We especially like peace and quiet; it makes us comfortable. But a prophetic view of the Messiah's work requires us to ask difficult questions, such as: Is our comfort really just complacency?

Karpen asks, "What kind of peace are we willing to accept, even embrace, in the interest of being comfortable? A peace that demands no justice. A peace that makes peace with the exploitation of the poor. A peace that makes peace with our consumer culture; a peace that makes peace with the marginalization of anyone who's different. A peace that makes peace with a political system corrupted by money and distorted by partisan politics. Jesus is the Prince of Peace, the peace that the scripture tells us surpasses understanding. That is not peace at all costs, at any price."

A popular bumper sticker reads, "No Justice, No Peace." If John the Baptist lived today, I don't think he'd have a car—he'd be too quirky and nonconformist for that. But I think he'd like that bumper sticker, because his role in the story of the Messiah was to disturb any complacency masquerading as peace.

When Advent arrives and we're trying so hard to get comfortable for Christmas, no wonder we make sure John never shows up in the Christmas pageants!

PRAYER

Holy Spirit, help us remember that you are not Santa Claus. May that awareness help us to better appreciate the message of the prophets of old, such as John the Baptist, to remake our lives in your service.

REFLECTION

1. How can we observe Christmas in such a way as to preserve some of the family traditions and gift giving while still remembering the radical mission of the Savior?

2. The liturgical color for Advent and Lent is the same—purple. How are the two seasons alike and how are they different in their treatment of repentance?

3. What contemporary persons remind you of John the Baptist?

SATURDAY

~

How Much Is Too Much?

> *All we like sheep have gone astray;*
> *we have all turned to our own way,*
> *and the LORD has laid on him*
> *the iniquity of us all.*

> ISAIAH 53:6

Simplify your life. I heard a television evangelist preaching that advice this morning. Ah, I must admit, this is an area in which I can be described as one of little faith. I find it difficult to believe that simplification can happen in our country anytime soon, especially at Christmastime.

Despite our First Amendment, which states that Congress shall make no law establishing a religion, we do have a national religion in the United States. And it's not some kind of intolerant, right-wing fundamentalism, as those on the Left might charge. Neither is it the secular humanism against which the Right has railed for all these years.

No, both of those ideologies pale in comparison with the creeping power of our true national religion: consumerism.

Every day in this country we are told we need to buy something, which simply is untrue. If we're honest, we have many days when we don't *have* to spend money to acquire another item.

The disease of consumerism pervades all segments of our society. Its symptoms are obvious, whether you're at a trendy shop in Manhattan or one of the hundreds of Wal-Marts spread across small-town, rural, and suburban America.

Author Denise Roy tells the story of hearing a radio interview with a Tibetan monk who was asked to compare life in Tibet with life in the United States. He pointed out that life in Tibet is scheduled around prayer—and remarked that it's hard to adjust to a life built around shopping.

Clearly, gifts are not bad—whether receiving them or giving them. So, at what point does the way we mark Christmas get out of control and become destructive, even inimical to the message of the Messiah? Not an easy question, and one whose answer varies with each of us. Perhaps our dilemma stems from the fact that in this country we have a pretty good idea of what is not enough—but no sense of what is too much.

PRAYER

O God, from whom all blessings flow, temper our unchecked impulses to accumulate. Make us aware that less can be more—and can lead to more faith and greater trust in your providence.

REFLECTION

1. Americans are constantly told that a booming retail economy benefits the most people. What reasons might there be to question consumer spending?

2. Think of Presidents Reagan and Clinton. Eighties and nineties; old and young; Republican, Democrat; conservative, moderately liberal. Yet both promoted and rode the wave of a rip-roaring economy. In a country that views accumulation of possessions as beneficial, how can consumerism be curbed?

Third Week
OF
Advent

SUNDAY

❧

Courage

Surely he has borne our infirmities
*   and carried our diseases;*
yet we accounted him stricken,
*   struck down by God and afflicted.*
But he was wounded for our transgressions,
*   crushed for our iniquities;*
upon him was the punishment that made us whole,
and by his bruises we are healed.

ISAIAH 53:4-5

Bearing sorrows, shouldering heavy burdens—this theme shows up repeatedly in scripture and gets mentioned virtually every day in our lives. Dealing with hard times is part of life. We all know people who bear such unspeakable pain that we're almost embarrassed to complain about our own little discomforts.

When I began this Advent project in 1997, I remember reading a column by a man I always considered a colleague and friend. Jerry Thompson worked for

The Tennessean newspaper in Nashville for almost forty years as a reporter and later as a columnist. Within the journalism community of Middle Tennessee, we'd occasionally cross paths. I interviewed Jerry once for a series I was preparing on the Ku Klux Klan.

Thompson knew that subject well because he had infiltrated the Klan over a period of eighteen months during the late 1970s. As a result of his undercover work, Thompson wrote an award-winning series of articles and a book. But Jerry Thompson's greatest writing came during his battle with cancer. Thompson always wrote optimistically about his struggle. Yet, one memorable day in December 1997, his column was notably somber.

Thompson told his readers how, about eight months earlier, his previous treatment simply stopped working. The next few months brought the discovery of a new tumor, followed by round-the-clock chemotherapy and radiation treatments.

Thompson called this column a combination Christmas card and love letter to his many readers. He thanked them for their support, gave them (and their prayers) credit for the fact that he was still alive, and expressed gratitude for his large extended family and all the other blessings of his life.

Jerry could be folksy, a little vulgar, almost a "good ole boy" at times. Once, during a particularly difficult period of his cancer battle when the prognosis looked grim, Thompson wrote that he was no longer buying green bananas. Always a journalist with a conscience, he demonstrated fierce loyalty to ordinary people, the poor, and the powerless.

Today I'm thinking about Jerry and all the millions of other people throughout the world who must wake each morning and face insidious, persistent, incurable disease. What does the concept of Emmanuel—God with us—mean to them? Do they draw any comfort from knowing God has stood by them and provided strength and courage and guidance to them and their doctors through the struggle?

Or are there moments when *Emmanuel* seems like a mocking word? Does the all-powerful God really care about us and love us as children? Is it possible that God will answer our prayers and bring the peace of a cure?

Jerry Thompson died in January 2000, almost twelve years after his first cancer diagnosis. His life and struggle against cancer can only be described as a triumph. But writing those words, even though I'm certain they're true, makes me feel uncomfortably smug, philosophizing about a crisis I've never had to weather myself.

PRAYER

Eternal God, guide us never to slander you by telling those who suffer that their pain is "God's will." Instead, help us to be instruments and examples through which suffering people may feel your comfort.

REFLECTION

1. Discuss, if relevant, how you, your family, or close friends dealt with terminal illness.

2. In an interview on September 11, 2002, a woman widowed by the World Trade Center attacks one year earlier remarked that she's weary of hearing people tell her she must have faith. She said it's easy to lose faith. How does that reality inform the way we minister to people in the midst of tragedy?

MONDAY

White Supremacy

You shall break them with a rod of iron,
and dash them in pieces like a potter's vessel.

PSALM 2:9

Today I read a newspaper story about an incident at a hospital in Nashville that I simply cannot get off my mind. A woman with a heart ailment, accompanied by her husband, went to a doctor at Saint Thomas Hospital. After an examination, tests, and consultation, the doctor advised surgery, and the couple agreed.

Then the patient's husband issued a demand to the physician: No African-American man should be allowed in the operating room during his wife's surgery. Regardless of whether he was a surgeon, nurse, anesthesiologist, or medical technician, any African-American male assigned to the operating room for that woman's surgery would have to be replaced. The husband was adamant that his wife could not be seen naked by a black man.

On the day of the operation, the surgeon complied with the man's wishes and asked an African-American male technician to leave the room. The surgeon later formally apologized for his mistake.

The depth of racism is breathtaking. It's staggering to think that a husband whose wife clearly needed major, perhaps lifesaving, surgery would be so blinded by racism as to make such a request to a physician. I wonder what God must think when witnessing such bigotry, knowing that we all really are brothers and sisters, whether or not we admit that fact. Why such a visceral reaction to people of another skin color? Why such a desire to dominate?

In Mark, the shortest and most unadorned of the four accounts of Jesus' ministry, Jesus says at one point, "Repent, and believe in the good news" (1:15).

Further details are unnecessary.

PRAYER

God of justice, keep us mindful of the simple prayer of the tax collector, "Be merciful to me, a sinner!" Help us display the same humility.

REFLECTION

1. How do you think Christianity should impact our view of skin color?

2. While people of all ethnic groups are prone to bigotry as a legacy of sin, "white supremacy" has certainly often been institutionalized—slavery, colonialism, and segregation from South Africa to Alabama. Why do you think these institutions existed alongside the institutionalized Christian church?

TUESDAY

❧

Mom

For the trumpet will sound, and the dead will be raised imperishable, and we will be changed.

1 CORINTHIANS 15:52

No matter how I might choose to identify Advent and Christmas of 2000, I will always remember this as my first Christmas on earth without my mother.

Mom died in August after almost a decade of declining health, a short illness, and a valiant attempt at life-saving heart surgery. As a middle-aged man, I can hardly be surprised about having to bury a parent. So when people asked how I was, I tried to be accurate and tell them that my mother's death did not leave me devastated but surely diminished. The finality hit me especially hard midway through Advent when I stopped by the cemetery to see, for the first time, Mom's stone grave marker, which we had chosen in September but which had not been installed until shortly after Thanksgiving.

Death, especially the passing of someone as close as a mother, can leave surviving loved ones feeling melancholy and reflective. As I went through that Advent season, trying to maintain a perceptive and prayerful mind and paying special attention to the scripture, chosen by the poet Charles Jennens, on which Handel built *Messiah*, I found myself returning again and again to Paul's first letter to the Corinthians.

The image of the trumpet as a means of both waking the dead and heralding the arrival of a king or judge has endured for many centuries. It shows up in Paul's letters to the church at Thessalonica (1 Thess. 4:13-18). In the mid-1960s, I served funeral masses as an altar boy. Thirty-five years later, I still remember that scripture word for word. So when Mom died, and my sister and I had the chance to select some Bible verses to be read at her funeral, I chose that passage.

Something about the last section of Handel's oratorio, which contains more of the spirit of Easter than of Christmas or Advent, reassures the listener. This portion of the oratorio doesn't deal with the Messiah's earthly work—overturning injustice and changing systems so that they more equitably distribute the fruits of the earth from the haves to the have-nots. Neither does it speak of the personal repentance always involved in the

Messiah's call. All this is important—indispensable, really—to our growth as disciples of Jesus.

But this section offers another image of the Messiah: the Lamb who triumphed over death, through whose power we can do the same. During that Advent season, in a year of transition for my family following my mother's death, this image of Messiah provided tremendous comfort.

PRAYER

Great God, as we pray throughout our lives for a radical trust in you, grant that we might also possess that trust when we need it most—at the end.

REFLECTION

1. What do Christians mean when we say we believe in the resurrection of the body?

2. Do you think our belief that God has "prepared a place for us" makes the question of what happens to our bodies after death unimportant? Why or why not?

WEDNESDAY

 ∿

Bread of Life

*"Worthy is the Lamb that was slaughtered
to receive power and wealth and wisdom and might
and honor and glory and blessing!"*

REVELATION 5:12

W hen I think of Jesus as Lamb, I inevitably remember my childhood in Catholic churches, serving Mass as an altar boy, and hearing what was called, in those last days of the Latin Mass, the Agnus Dei. The words mean "Lamb of God," and they are said just before the sharing of the bread and wine.

Jesus as Lamb and Bread of Life. Those words took on new meaning for me during a mission trip to Honduras in February and March 1999. Our group's assignment was a construction project on the island of Roatán—helping to build a school. On a Saturday morning about midway through the mission trip, several of us took a ferry over to the mainland to the coastal city

of La Ceiba. We had heard from several fellow mission-
ers about a ministry called the Bread of Life.

The people of the Zion Church run the program on
Saturdays. Volunteers arrive early to begin preparing
lunch for the guests who will arrive at noon. Most of
these folks are homeless; many are women with young
children. In the winter of 1999, Honduras was just a few
months past the devastation of Hurricane Mitch, which
had killed thousands and left even more with nothing.

The first business of the day for the guests is listening to a fiery sermon. Then it's time for lunch.

After spending the morning helping with prepara-
tion, now we will help serve the meal. It's not much of a
meal, to be honest. Everyone will get a small bowl half-
filled with soup. The soup contains rice, a few vegeta-
bles, and chicken flavor—for some lucky people, maybe
even a scrap of meat. Each person gets one tortilla and
a cup of fruit juice. More than a hundred people have
come on this hot, sunny Saturday. In what is statistically
the third-poorest country in the Western Hemisphere,
these folks are among the worst off.

It is a sacred moment to be at La Ceiba's Bread of
Life service, to help prepare and serve the meal. We're
not doing this to ease some kind of middle-class guilt or
to earn "points" with God, as if we could do that.

No, the privilege of serving comes, I think, from the
simple experience of participating in the work of the
Messiah. This is the Messiah who feels special solidarity

with the poor, who works to overturn systems where justice does not prevail, who brings the beggar Lazarus into his kingdom, into the bosom of Abraham even as the rich man, Dives, stands far away, pleading for entry (Luke 16:19-31).

We won't solve the problems of injustice, inequality, racism, and consumerism this Christmas season—or in my lifetime or yours. But if we know what has been said about the Messiah, then we should also recognize how we need to spend our time and our treasure.

We should also realize that the commercial onslaught during the weeks preceding the holiday that marks our Messiah's birth really has nothing to do with him at all.

PRAYER

God of the poor, the hungry, and the forgotten, remind us of your special preference for those who suffer. Inspire us to work for justice.

REFLECTION

1. What responsibility does the United States bear for the fact that Honduras is the third-poorest country in the Western Hemisphere?

2. People just beginning volunteer work often say, "I get more than I give," a statement that can be inspiring

and is usually accurate. Discuss how this statement can also be self-centered.

3. We all know people who have broken the barriers of their comfort zones—Mother Teresa, Albert Schweitzer, and Dorothy Day are famous examples. Why is admiring them so automatic but emulating them so difficult?

THURSDAY

~

Beneath Hallowed Ground

*Listen, I will tell you a mystery! We will not all die,
but we will all be changed, in a moment, in the twinkling of an eye, at the last trumpet.*

1 CORINTHIANS 15:51-52

I work in Lower Manhattan, three streets from the site
where the twin towers of the World Trade Center
stood. As I write this meditation, almost eleven months
have elapsed since the terrorist attacks.

Several subway lines in New York City run near that
sixteen-acre site. The 1/9 route was most directly affected,
its final three stations closed by damage. Repairing that
tunnel took more than a year.

However, another subway line—the N and R—provides me with one of the countless powerful feelings
that seem to have engulfed New Yorkers in a continuous
wave this past year.

The N and R trains run their usual routes, but there
is one station where they do not stop—Cortlandt

Street—on the eastern perimeter of what has become internationally known as Ground Zero.

The station and platform appear to be structurally sound, but there is no way to exit to the street on the southbound side because of the recovery and reconstruction effort. So, for eleven months, riders traveling on the N and R between City Hall and Rector Street have passed through a station in which time has stood still since that sunny, awful Tuesday morning. The turnstiles are there, as are the MetroCard self-service machines and the booths where the transit workers took money for fares. All appear undamaged.

Riding through that station evokes an ethereal feeling in me. Although I'm a voracious reader and use commuting time to catch up, I stop what I am doing when the train passes through Cortlandt Street. I sense a moment, a day, frozen in time, but there's a lot more than that. As we travel through that station, I think of what happened just above me, how almost twenty-eight hundred human beings stopped living within a period of 102 minutes, most of them dying in the final minutes when the towers fell.

As Saint Paul wrote—and as Handel and his librettist, Charles Jennens, quoted—"We will all be changed, in a moment, in the twinkling of an eye."

Even now, a year later, less than half of those killed in Lower Manhattan on September 11 have been positively identified. Many more than a thousand people vanished without a trace—their mortal remains, at least. Their spirits—well, they're out there somewhere, still dwelling with us, if we can imagine the "big picture."

On a normal day, it's not unusual for me to pass by Ground Zero three or four times, either at street level or via the subway. Often I must negotiate my way through the growing crowds of tourists who flock like pilgrims to what has become a sacred place.

For months, whether walking or riding, I have practiced a ritual as I pass—reciting the final section of the Apostles' Creed: "I believe in the Holy Spirit, the holy catholic church, the communion of saints, the forgiveness of sins, the resurrection of the body, and the life everlasting."[1]

Especially "the communion of saints." This phrase reminds me that I am wrong to write "more than a thousand people vanished without a trace."

Ground Zero also helps us remember that. So does the Messiah.

PRAYER

Eternal rest grant to them, O Lord, and let perpetual light shine upon them.

---

1. Some churches substitute *universal* for *catholic*.

REFLECTION

1. One rabbi described the multiple disasters of September 11, 2001, as God-free events. What do you think of that description?

2. Also in response to September 11, 2001, many said, "It must have been God's will, because so much good came out of it." Do you agree with both halves of that statement, one half, or neither?

FRIDAY

Putting Scissors to the Bible

For I know that my Redeemer lives,
and that at the last he will stand upon
the earth;
and after my skin has been thus destroyed,
then in my flesh I will see God.

JOB 19:25-26

Back in the mid-1990s, when we still lived in Nashville and when our two older sons, Dan and Matt, were teenagers, our family participated in a program that brings Catholic and Protestant adolescents from Northern Ireland to the United States for a month to live and interact with American teens and, more important, with each other.

One day, I asked several of these young people if they'd like to spend the next day on a field trip—I offered to take them to see some of the sights of Middle Tennessee. I was thinking perhaps they'd like to visit the Hermitage, the home of President Andrew Jackson;

Mammoth Cave, a hundred miles up the road in Kentucky; maybe the Civil War battlefield in nearby Franklin; or even a professional baseball game.

"What sounds good to you?" I asked.

"Can we go to the mall?" came the unanimous answer.

I have traveled enough to know that a huge attraction of the United States is its economic wealth—the quality and especially the seemingly endless quantity of consumer goods. But I worry about how that condition affects our country's value system.

That incident came to mind again when I read a story about a seminary experiment, told by the Reverend Jim Wallis, cofounder of the Sojourners movement. A group of seminary students decided to go through the Bible, all sixty-six books, and chronicle every reference to the poor. They found that in the Hebrew Scriptures (Old Testament) the poor, and service to the poor, is the second most frequently mentioned topic. Idolatry is first. In the Christian Scriptures (New Testament), the results are even more dramatic.

The seminarians found that, in the New Testament, one of every sixteen verses refers to the poor. Among the four Gospels, the ratio is one of every ten. In the Gospel of Luke, it's one of every seven. In the epistle of James, one of every five.

Then one seminarian had the idea to take a pair of scissors to the Bible, cutting out every reference to the poor. As you can imagine, not much of the Bible remained. Cutting out the poor leaves the Bible in tatters, reduces it to shreds. The Messiah celebrated in Isaiah and in Handel's great oratorio is a God with special preference for the poor.[1]

As Christ's followers—those who have committed to share in the work of the Messiah—we must constantly remind ourselves of that preference. And in a consumeristic world, during a blessed season when commercial temptations often reach their highest level, such reminders become even more critical.

PRAYER

Almighty God, remind us how often scripture mentions the poor, and help us remember that we also should give them priority. Help us to speak and act on behalf of those whose voices our society often ignores.

REFLECTION

1. Now that you've seen the numbers, what do all these scriptural references to the poor mean to you?

2. The often-quoted verse "the poor you will always have with you" (NIV) is generally used out of context. Read Mark 14:3-9 and see if the phrase takes on a different meaning.

---

1. Jim Wallis, *The Soul of Politics: Beyond "Religious Right" and "Secular Left"* (San Diego, Calif.: Harcourt Brace & Co., 1995), 178.

SATURDAY

~

God's Citizenship

Why do the nations conspire
and the peoples plot in vain?
The kings of the earth set themselves,
and the rulers take counsel together,
against the LORD and his anointed.

PSALM 2:1-2

Less than two weeks after the attacks on the World Trade Center, I spoke with a minister from Buffalo who was here in New York City doing relief work. He told me that it upset him to see so many New Yorkers wearing flag pins and to see the Stars and Stripes flying from so many buildings. He felt these were nationalistic and inappropriate responses.

At the time, I politely and gently recommended that maybe he should wait awhile before judging. The events of 9/11 traumatized New Yorkers. After all, the mass murder of twenty-eight hundred people takes a long time to process. Besides, Manhattan is a small island,

and the attacks didn't miss any of us by much. I suggested that the flag had become a coping mechanism for many folks and a symbol of angry jingoism for only a relative few.

I still believe that. However, some cultural phenomena that have emerged since September 11 present challenges for those of us who would follow the path of the Messiah born that night in Bethlehem.

Take, for example, the song "God Bless America." The Irving Berlin classic from the late 1930s became ubiquitous after the terror attacks—at baseball games, at awards banquets, on the radio and television.

Asking God to bless America is a wonderful idea, but it doesn't go far enough. We must ask God to bless not only America—North and South—but also Asia, Africa, Australia, Antarctica, and Europe. And here's the really difficult part: We must ask God to bless Afghanistan, Iraq, Palestine, Israel, Iran, North Korea, and members of al-Qaida.

Although God stood with us on that terrible day and in the months that followed, God is not a U.S. citizen. God is not an American and certainly not a Democrat or a Republican.

During this season as we prepare for the Messiah, let's do the hard work of transformation, including changing any subtle assumptions we may not even realize we have. Sing "God Bless America." It's an important prayer, a worthy petition. But don't stop there.

Dr. Jeremiah Wright of Trinity United Church of Christ in Chicago said it best in a televised sermon when he reminded us that we won't find the words *God bless America* in the scriptures.

What we will find, in John 3:16, is "God so loved the *world*."

PRAYER

Heavenly God, Jesus said, "Pray for those who persecute you." It must have been difficult for humankind to hear this command then, and it's tough for us to hear it now. But help us to listen—and obey.

REFLECTION

1. After September 11, 2001, more than one person (both lay and clergy) said, "God got our attention." How do you feel about the image of a God who views the horrifying, painful deaths of nearly three thousand people as a way to "get our attention"?

2. How might the idea that a country is blessed evolve into the idea that the country is favored?

Fourth Week
of
Advent

SUNDAY

~

Jesus Sightings

*Then I heard what seemed to be the voice of a great
multitude, like the sound of many waters and like the
sound of mighty thunderpeals, crying out,*
  "Hallelujah!
  *For the Lord our God the Almighty reigns." . . .
On his robe and on his thigh he has a name
inscribed, "King of kings and Lord of lords."*

Som
REVELATION 19:6, 16

Back in the final months of 1999, as I stood in a super-
market checkout line, I noticed a headline in a
tabloid newspaper: "Jesus Sightings Increase As Millen-
nium Approaches."

Far be it from me to question the accuracy of any
newspaper headline! But it did occur to me that "Jesus
sightings" have been happening for a long time.

On that first Easter afternoon, no more than twelve
to fourteen hours after the Resurrection, two disciples
walking on the road to Emmaus experienced a lengthy

Jesus sighting, complete with extended conversation and culminating in a dinner invitation.

Of course, as seems to be characteristic of human-kind, the two disciples never recognized their experience as a "Jesus sighting" until it was over. Let's face it, we all experience "Jesus sightings" regularly—the homeless man shaking a cup on the street in hopes that we'll drop in a coin, the elderly homebound person who needs our companionship, the family struggling to communicate with some government agency despite a language barrier.

Jesus knows we have difficulty recognizing these "sightings," but what he says on the subject in Matthew 25 does not exactly reassure us. From reading the passage, it seems as though the ability to recognize Jesus in these everyday sightings is the very key to where we spend eternity.

Why do we so often miss these sightings? Maybe because we limit our thinking about the coming of the Messiah to only two possibilities: Jesus as a baby in Bethlehem and Jesus in glory at the end of earthly time.

But the Resurrection unleashed the power of Jesus here, in the world, right now. That power enables his disciples to tell people of his radical gospel; it ensures that the kingdom of God is at hand; it gives us life more abundant.

It's possible, I suppose, to see Christianity as a lifeboat that only a dedicated few can board to ride across the lake to safety. But surely there is another perspective, as Anglican priest and author David Winter has pointed out—that the Messiah has won a great and lasting victory over evil and that we are not a small, almost defeated, barely rescued remnant but rather the vanguard of a huge harvest.

I guess your view depends on whether you're a pessimist or an optimist. I find myself agreeing with David Winter: The Christian faith should make us optimists.

PRAYER

Loving God, may our faith in your ultimate plan make us not only optimists but also eager workers for the great harvest that is to come.

REFLECTION

1. How do we maintain balance between a personal relationship with Jesus and the social covenant to which we are called as coworkers of the Messiah?

2. How do we ensure that our concept of a personal relationship does not become belief in a "private salvation deal"?

3. Does your faith in God make you an optimist, a pessimist, or something in between?

MONDAY

❧

Looking for the Lost

In that region there were shepherds living in the fields,
keeping watch over their flock by night. Then an
angel of the Lord stood before them, and the glory of
the Lord shone around them, and they were terrified.
LUKE 2:8-9

Sometimes a coincidence is so powerful and relevant
that we begin to wonder if it's really a coincidence.

The Gospel reading specified in the three-year lec-
tionary used by most mainline Christian churches in the
United States for Sunday, September 16, 2001, came
from Luke 15:1-10. This passage contains the story of
the lost sheep—the shepherd who leaves ninety-nine to
search for one sheep, the shepherd who goes looking
for the lost.

It is impossible to describe the power of this story
on that Sunday in the city of New York. For weeks and
even months after September 11, as we walked the
streets of New York, we saw faces, usually smiling at us,

on simple posters and handbills hanging from utility poles, benches, phone booths, fences, sides of buildings—any available public surface.

These faces were everywhere, although more concentrated in the areas where street memorials sprang up, such as Union Square, Saint Paul's Chapel, and the Armory at 26th Street and Lexington Avenue where a family assistance center operated for a time.

Under the pictures, beneath the faces, was information—birthdate, clothes each person had been wearing on the morning of September 11, perhaps the location of a birthmark or tattoo.

The handbills listed a floor of the towers, almost always a high floor, where the person smiling out at us had worked or was last seen. And, finally, of course, a phone number to call with any information.

Someone estimated that there were ninety thousand of these posters and handbills in New York City. I believe it. Ninety thousand posters "looking for the lost."

In a city where, by necessity, we all live a large part of our lives in public spaces (parks, sidewalks, buses, subways), the enormity of the loss was seen everywhere.

Ninety thousand posters, almost all of them containing smiling faces. Faces of every hue, connected with names from Asia, Europe, Africa, Latin America, the United States.

Of all the words written or spoken on and after September 11, many of them terribly profound and meaningful, three brief sentences stand out for me.

On Thursday, September 13, several television and radio stations broadcast an interview with a woman outside a comfort center where relatives were instructed to go to seek information on their missing family members.

"I just have to know he's all right. If he's alive, I want to know he's all right. If he's dead, at least I know he's all right."

Her last sentence is most powerful.

In a terrible time, perhaps without even thinking about what she said, that woman had spoken a statement of faith.

The Messiah is not one-dimensional. A comforter of the poor, certainly. A prophet to challenge the powerful, without question. A transformer of people and society, oh yes.

But also a shepherd who never stops looking for the lost.

PRAYER

God our Shepherd, during times of unfathomable pain we draw on the reserves of faith we may not even realize we have. Thank you for those reserves, and remind us often of the importance of nurturing the seeds of faith inside us.

REFLECTION

1. What role do you think God plays in times of unspeakable horror?

2. A widow of September 11 says, "Don't tell me about God—my husband was murdered and disappeared without a trace." How can Christians authentically and yet compassionately do the work of God when we encounter someone in terrible pain?

TUESDAY

❧

To Walk and Not Faint

He was despised and rejected by others;
a man of suffering and acquainted with
infirmity.

ISAIAH 53:3

While moving boxes from a closet recently, I found some old journals I kept during overseas trips. Rereading such notes is instructive because we can get comfortable here in the United States and forget the daily struggle of life in other places—and what a privilege and honor it is to serve others.

In 1987 I spent eight days in Haiti. Best known now, unfortunately, for its poverty, Haiti is also a country of proud people who will—and should—remind visitors that theirs is the second nation (after the United States) in the Western Hemisphere to gain independence by revolting against a European colonial power, and the first independent nation in the hemisphere to abolish slavery.

Poverty in Haiti, then and now, cannot be measured by any of the usual standards, even in the developing world. On Palm Sunday afternoon, our missions group got the chance to visit the Hospital for the Dying.

Run by Mother Teresa's Missionaries of Charity, the hospital—really not much more than a ward—provides care for people who will not get better, who often have been left out on the street to die.

Sister Rose from St. Louis escorted us past the cots, thirty to a room, and the patients, some who were as young as their mid-twenties. I remember their vacant stares, their legs covered with sores, their lungs racked by tuberculosis, their bodies succumbing to AIDS, or SIDA as it's known there.

In the midst of such a scene, I don't know how a particular patient can stand out, but one man did. His body curled into a fetal position, he was less than four feet from head to toe. A sheet barely covered his nakedness, and only an IV kept him alive.

My two companions and I were cowards. We stayed about thirty minutes and left, saying "bonsoir" to all, an inadequate statement.

Before we left, though, we spoke briefly with the sisters, seven of them, who serve in that hospital all day, every day, without any hope that the situation will improve. They provide care for these people because they believe their patients deserve to die with a trace of dignity—and love.

In another part of Port-au-Prince, we met a man from Wisconsin who ran a medical clinic. On the nearby island of La Gonâve, a frail Michigan man pushing eighty made two harrowing fifteen-mile weekly trips, across often rough seas, to bring grain and beans to the people of the island where he had lived for fifteen years.

At the time, I remember thinking, *There is no logical reason to live and serve in Haiti.* One of the sisters told us that the grace of God gave them the strength to start again each morning.

Fifteen years later, I'm still not sure how they do it. But I have a better idea of why. The call of the gospel is powerful; when we answer, the hard work has just begun!

We commit not only to change our own lives but also to work to accomplish a vision—transforming the world. Service to others lies at the center of that vision.

Perhaps that's the thought we should keep in mind as Christmas approaches. And if the idea of a Messiah who might ask us to serve God's children in that most difficult mission field of Haiti shakes up our schedule of Christmas shopping and holiday parties, maybe that's the best Christmas gift we'll ever get.

PRAYER

God of eternity, help our much smaller minds to remember that the value lies in the journey, not the destination—and in the hard work of service, not necessarily in the solution of problems of injustice.

REFLECTION

1. We often feel the understandable impulse to help people, solve problems, and move on to the next task. How does a place like Haiti prove we can't always do that?

2. We may respond to overwhelming need by throwing up our hands in despair and saying we can't change certain situations, not even in a lifetime. Do you agree or disagree with that statement? Does it matter that we may not be able to change situations in our lifetime?

WEDNESDAY

Winter Solstice

Who is this King of glory?
The LORD of hosts, he is the King of glory.
PSALM 24:10

Winter solstice—the longest night of the year, following the shortest day. Ancient people placed great importance on this day. It must have terrified them at first, knowing that their very lives depended on that ball of fire in the sky that was visible for fewer and fewer hours every month. Then, when they had observed enough cycles to realize that the sun would reach its point of shortest duration and rebound again, the ancients celebrated the day. What they really celebrated was the sun as the source of life itself.

We know that the date for Christmas was set to coincide with Saturnalia, which in turn coincided with the winter solstice. So, for those of us living in the Northern Hemisphere, a reflection about the Messiah and light is completely appropriate.

I spent ninety minutes today walking around Inwood Hill Park on the northwest tip of Manhattan. New York City has many "green spaces," and most are beautiful, made more so by the fact that the city, especially Manhattan, contains so much concrete.

But whereas Central Park, for all its beauty, is a human-designed green space, Inwood Park is natural. The trees, the cliffs, and the nearby water are much the same as they were when Manhattan was a wilderness inhabited by Native Americans, decades before the Dutch made their alleged twenty-four-dollar purchase in 1626.

The trees are bare today. A two-inch blanket of snow covers the ground; a few squirrels race up and down the trunks with winter provisions in their mouths. Nature is not dead, however; it merely sleeps.

In the great circle of life, this is a predictable interval that will be followed by rebirth. There's a lesson for us here about patience. Spring will come.

For the Hebrew people in Babylon, exiled so long that some might have despaired of ever returning to Jerusalem, God's promises of comfort and of a Messiah, communicated through Isaiah, might have seemed like a cruel joke, unless they had patience. And faith.

Embracing the Messiah and setting your shoulder to the plow to do Messiah's work on earth also require patience. God's new world on earth, God's reclamation of us—all of us—won't likely be accomplished in our lifetimes. Again, doing the work requires perseverance.

Trusting in the ultimate result requires us to have the same quality the exiled Israelites needed—patience. And faith.

PRAYER

God of eternity, help us to develop perspective, the ability to see the big picture—the picture that, incidentally, does not feature our agenda at the center of the universe.

REFLECTION

1. In a society of cell phones, e-mail, PalmPilots, and high-speed travel, not only is patience hard to find, it's not even necessarily encouraged. Discuss the implications of this statement.

2. How do we strike a balance between patience and the urgent needs of people—in other words, how do we keep patience from becoming complacency?

THURSDAY

❧

Traveling Light

"For my yoke is easy, and my burden is light."
MATTHEW 11:30

There are some rewards to getting out of bed and traveling at 4:20 A.M. on a wintry morning when the wind chill is measured in negative numbers.

Like sitting in a moving train and looking out a window to the east. I see bare trees rising out of a blanket of snow; the horizon fades from pink to blue to white; a waning crescent moon rides high above that horizon.

I am traveling two days before Christmas. This scene of great natural beauty is not the only gift I will receive this morning.

Before boarding the train, I stand in the main Amtrak concourse of New York City's Pennsylvania Station with thousands of holiday pilgrims. Scores, perhaps even hundreds of us, are southbound this morning.

Many appear to be in their late teens and early twenties, most likely college students headed home for the winter break. A great number are African Americans, boarding a train that will stop in the towns and cities of the South: Fredericksburg, Kannapolis, and Greensboro—where their parents and grandparents came from in the great northern migration of the early twentieth century.

These sights and, of course, this time of year make me think of the power of culture, almost always stronger than ideology, even stronger than religion. Ritual, custom, and tradition are among the raw materials of culture.

In the United States, Christmas carries more ritual, custom, and tradition than just about any other day. Coming at the end of our calendar, Christmas is a signpost. Not only do we celebrate, but we also take stock and note the passing of time and the sure, irreversible ebbing of our lives.

Taking stock. It's almost impossible to overstate the importance of that practice. Evaluation is a task we should do more frequently than just at year's end. We have a habit of filling our closets, accumulating much that, upon taking stock, may prove not only unnecessary but also difficult to carry.

Perhaps that's why God would not let the Israelites collect more than one day's worth of manna (except on the day before the Sabbath). Maybe it's why the man in Luke 12 who fills his barn with grain, then dies the same night, is often called the rich fool. Or why Jesus challenges those of us with two coats to give one away.

Taking stock—really, seriously taking stock—often motivates us to "travel light." It forces us to travel with fewer possessions and more trust.

It also leaves us in a much better position to recognize and welcome the new world of the Messiah and that work of which we should be a part.

PRAYER

Heavenly God, remind us that we are born with nothing and we leave this earth with nothing. May this knowledge encourage us to work for causes that will transcend our short time on earth and leave a lasting legacy.

REFLECTION

1. Traveling light sounds good in theory, but sometimes it's difficult to practice. How do you feel about parting with possessions when you clean out a closet?

2. Have you ever moved to a new home and found a box that had remained unopened since your last move? What does such a discovery reveal about baggage we keep but no longer need?

FRIDAY

∾

Not a Silent Night

But the angel said to them, "Do not be afraid; for
see—I am bringing you good news of great joy for
all the people: to you is born this day in the city of
David a Savior, who is the Messiah, the Lord."

LUKE 2:10-11

I love singing Christmas carols. The composers of those
great songs of the season have every right to employ
literary license. But I wonder if any carol contains more
exaggerated literary license than "Silent Night."

I have read surveys reporting that "Silent Night" is
the favorite Christmas carol of all time, at least in the
United States. To my untrained voice, "Silent Night"
remains a difficult song to sing. But whenever I contem-
plate the lyrics, I always think of the late CBS and ABC
news correspondent Harry Reasoner and a wonderfully
perceptive radio commentary he delivered about twenty
years ago.

Reasoner stated, with all due respect, that the first Christmas was not and could not have been a "silent night." I agree, and I think any Advent reflection on the meaning of the Messiah should explore this idea.

Bethlehem must have been bedlam that night. The town was packed with its own residents and hundreds, maybe thousands of travelers. Everyone was there for the census, which could not have been very popular, since that pagan emperor in Rome had ordered it.

As the time gets later and the sun goes down and people realize that Bethlehem has insufficient lodging to accommodate all the visitors, you can be sure that tempers flared. Between husband and wife, between visitor and innkeeper, maybe even between Mary and Joseph. The last days of pregnancy can test the patience of a saint, even two saints, especially a couple facing a night in a cave or stable.

We can be sure that the wonderful, distinctive commerce of the Middle East was in high gear and full voice that night—merchants offering their products and, ten feet away, a competitor hawking his own merchandise at a slightly lower price as would-be buyers shout back and forth in an attempt to negotiate a better deal.

And, yes, it's safe to say that "ladies of the evening" stood in the shadows, available for a fee to some out-of-towners stuck in Bethlehem at the behest of the emperor. Reasoner concluded his commentary by noting that, in Bethlehem that evening, it was *not* a silent night. It couldn't have been. Otherwise, there would have been no need for redemption.

We must never sanitize the night or the world into which the Messiah came. A world not silent but very much in need of redemption. Just like the world into which he comes today.

PRAYER

Almighty God, help us remember that although that night in Bethlehem was the turning point of history, it did not immediately change the human heart. Such change takes time and work—our work.

REFLECTION

1. What image have you held of that night in Bethlehem? How does it make you feel to think of mundane, even seedy, activities happening just a few hundred yards from where the Messiah was born?

2. What do you think of the statement "The church should not be a museum for saints but a hospital for sinners"?

CHRISTMAS EVE

∾

Rewriting the Story

Suddenly there was with the angel a multitude of
the heavenly host, praising God and saying,
  "Glory to God in the highest heaven,
  and on earth peace among those whom he
    favors!"

LUKE 2:13-14

Christmas 1990 still ranks among my most memorable Christmases. Cheryl, our sons Dan and Matt, and I spent that Christmas Eve working in the homeless shelter of our church in Hermitage, Tennessee.

Our congregation put much effort into making this Christmas Eve special for our guests. The meal included many traditional holiday favorites such as ham and turkey, and our church members provided gifts for all the guests, especially the children. Everyone who worked that night mentioned how it seemed more meaningful because it was Christmas.

That shelter program in Nashville is called Room in the Inn. The Reverend Charles Strobel, a Catholic priest I mentioned earlier, organized the ministry. Strobel has a great perspective on what the homeless, or any people who are systematically marginalized, teach us about the Messiah. "Who realized that the baby in the manger, whose parents were turned away from lodging, was the Messiah?" he asks. "Only those with enough vision to believe that God is revealed in the stranger among them."

Strobel sees service to the homeless as an opportunity to rewrite the Christmas story. Instead of saying no, as did the Bethlehem innkeeper to Mary and Joseph, we can say yes to those who are rejected. More often than not, rejection is not a conscious action but rather a kind of terrible neglect.

In one of his sermons the Reverend Martin Luther King Jr. explored Luke's scripture about the rich man and Lazarus. King started out by looking almost sympathetically at the rich man; after all, he didn't really commit any sin, did he? That man, traditionally called Dives, suffered from a terrible blindness, a malady not particularly rare in our own world. As King put it, the rich man "never saw Lazarus, even though he passed him every day."

Thomas Merton wrote of Jesus: "His place is with those others who do not belong, who are rejected because they are regarded as weak; and with those who are discredited."[1]

It's easy for us to look at but never really see people around us who are different. Overlooking these people was also easy in Bethlehem that night of the census.

Because overlooking the marginalized is so easy, we must constantly recommit ourselves to rewriting the Christmas story in the name of the Messiah whose birth we celebrate.

PRAYER

Almighty God, you know that we all experience selective blindness, especially toward persons who need our attention the most. Cure us of our blindness and prepare us for your service.

REFLECTION

1. If Merton is correct and the Messiah's place is with those who do not belong, where does that leave us? Must we live on the margins to live authentically?

2. We speak of the poor as being first to recognize the Messiah. We also say they're so sincere, so innocent, so authentic, so caring and sharing. Why do we describe the poor in such a positive way yet work so hard to keep our distance from them?

---

1. Thomas Merton, "The Time of No Room," in *Watch for the Light: Readings for Advent and Christmas* (Farmington, Pa.: Plough Publishing House, 2001), December 31st entry.

CHRISTMAS DAY

⌒

A Dangerous World
Then and Now

*Now after they had left, an angel of the Lord
appeared to Joseph in a dream and said, "Get up,
take the child and his mother, and flee to Egypt, and
remain there until I tell you; for Herod is about to
search for the child, to destroy him."*

MATTHEW 2:13

T he Christmas season, especially as the comfortable
middle class of the United States observes it, can
easily lull us into warm, self-satisfied complacency. We
read the ancient scriptures each year and thrill at our
visions of the young family with their firstborn child in
a manger and cute animals all around, failing to register
how really uncomfortable, inconvenient, and smelly
that experience must have been.

We read descriptions of angels singing in the skies
and shepherds standing on hillsides watching them with
innocent, awestruck faces and then picture the shepherds

tromping over to the stable to see the baby. But we never give much thought to how a young mother who has just given birth under the toughest possible circumstances might react to such a visit (not with unbridled enthusiasm, I would think).

By reading those scriptures with a certain mind-set, we can easily ignore the rough edges of the Christmas story, the revolutionary message of the Messiah, the dangerous mission of the little babe.

Then we read the second chapter of Matthew, which is not part of Handel's oratorio but whose message is consistent with Messiah as a symbol of radical change. Now we know what the arrival of this baby boy means to the powerful, the entrenched, the selfish, and the greedy.

Herod, clearly disturbed by what he sees as a threat to his power and influence, tries to use the Magi to lay a trap for the child. Divine intervention in a dream foils Herod's plot and sends the king into a rage, a murderous fury. Young, innocent victims die bloody deaths. I remember the feast day for them in the Catholic Church of my childhood—the Feast of the Holy Innocents.

The young family, which already had endured so many hardships associated with a journey in late pregnancy and a birth among a group of farm animals, must now flee for their lives into a foreign land that has a long history of discord with their own nation.

The second chapter of the Gospel of Matthew is not a picture from Currier and Ives. It portrays a world of violence, deceit, and horrible injustice. Not so very different from the world in which we live today.

The Messiah came because that world needed, really needed, deliverance and redemption—it really needed a Messiah.

It still does.

PRAYER

God in heaven, open our eyes to the challenge of the Messiah, the danger of being authentic to his message, the reality of the cross, and the assurance that Christ makes the yoke easy and the burden light.

REFLECTION

1. Herod is easy to portray as a classic villain. In what ways does the message of the Messiah bring danger into our own lives and times?

2. How does an awareness of the rough edges of the Christmas story affect our experience of the holiday season?

ABOUT THE AUTHOR

J im Melchiorre, an Emmy Award–winning television journalist and producer, is a husband and father of three sons. He and his wife, Cheryl, live with their youngest son in New York City, where all are members of Saint Paul and Saint Andrew United Methodist Church.

Melchiorre holds a B.A. degree from Pennsylvania State University and a M.S. from Pace University. In addition to his many years as a journalist, Melchiorre served in the U.S. Navy and has been active in lay volunteer mission movements since the mid-1980s. He has traveled extensively in the United States and in more than two dozen foreign countries.

Reflections of Messiah is Jim's first book. Upper Room Books is pleased to offer this thoughtful collection of Advent meditations.

Other Advent Resources from Upper Room Books

WHILE WE WAIT

Living the Questions of Advent
by Mary Lou Redding

If you are looking for a unique group Advent study, *While We Wait* offers new ways of connecting study participants with their own faith questions. Readers have the chance to look at some biblical figures on whom we don't always focus during Advent: Tamar, Ruth, Mary, Zechariah, Elizabeth, and the Magi. Author Mary Lou Redding says this book allows for real-life struggles and questions as a legitimate part of Advent's spiritual exploration.

ISBN 0-8358-0982-X • Paperback • 136 pages

THE VIGIL

Keeping Watch in the
Season of Christ's Coming
by Wendy M. Wright

In captivating, powerful prose, Wendy Wright weaves together the threads of the liturgical calendar, traditions from medieval Christmas masses, and stories from scripture and her own life. A thought-provoking study for small groups or a delightful gift for those with whom we share the waiting and watching during the season of hope, *The Vigil* will be a blessed companion in the seasons of Advent, Christmas, and Epiphany.

ISBN 0-8358-0661-8 • Paperback • 176 pages

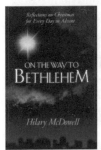

ON THE WAY TO BETHLEHEM

Reflections on Christmas
for Every Day in Advent
by Hilary McDowell

This series of daily readings creates a richly imaginative and interactive narrative that permits the reader to cast off emotional baggage, smell the hay and hear the thoughts of fellow seekers in the stable, listen to a shepherd's awe-filled story, and eventually encounter the Christ child himself. In the hands of skillful guide Hilary McDowell, Advent becomes a fresh, heartfelt experience, an impetus for setting forth on a journey to encounter Christ.

ISBN 0-8358-0920-X • Paperback • 160 pages

SETTING THE CHRISTMAS STAGE

Readings for the Advent Season
by John Indermark

In *Setting the Christmas Stage*, author John Indermark helps us find space for the spiritual journey of Advent, looking at the Christmas story as a dramatic and familiar pageant. As well as exploring the characters and settings that comprise the Christmas story, this book uses elements from the stage to view how Advent gradually pieces together plots, persons, and scenes in order to move the drama to its climax at Christmas.

ISBN 0-8358-0947-1 • Paperback • 128 pages

To order these and other Upper Room resources, call our Customer Service Center toll free at 1-800-972-0433 Monday through Friday, order online at www.upperroom.org/bookstore, or order through your local bookstore.

About Volunteers in Mission

‿

If you've read all or most of this Advent devotional guide, you've undoubtedly noticed numerous references to the United Methodist Volunteers in Mission (UMVIM) program.

UMVIM, which began in 1976, is a fellowship of believers, both lay and clergy, men and women, adults and youth—and not exclusively United Methodists—who step out in faith to serve the needs of people around the world. VIM serves people in the United States and overseas on assignments as short as one or two weeks and as long as two years.

Most volunteers work in construction, medicine, dentistry, optometry, and education.

I once mentioned to a friend that the five most significant experiences of my life were the birth of our three sons, a visit to the ancestral home in Italy of my immigrant grandparents, and my first Volunteers in Mission trip. I wasn't exaggerating.

If you'd like more information, please visit the UMVIM Web site at:

www.gbgm-umc.org/vim